Persis Chase

The Lancaster Sketch Book

Persis Chase

The Lancaster Sketch Book

ISBN/EAN: 9783744733243

Printed in Europe, USA, Canada, Australia, Japan

Cover: Foto ©Thomas Meinert / pixelio.de

More available books at **www.hansebooks.com**

The Lancaster Sketch Book

The Lancaster Sketch Book

BY

PERSIS F. CHASE.

"There lies a village in a peaceful vale
With sloping hills and waving woods around."

BRATTLEBORO, VT. :
FRANK E. HOUSH & CO., PUBLISHERS.
1887.

F 44
.L2 4

PREFACE.

Most of the following articles appeared in the columns of the Lancaster *Gazette*, with the exception of some of the sketches which were published in the Portland *Transcript*.

It is hoped they will prove acceptable in the more pretentious form of a book, to the residents of the town; and perhaps those whose former home was in this locality, but who have wandered far away from this pleasant valley among the mountains, will recall the scenes of other days in reading these sketches; and the summer visitor who has found health and pleasure among our hills, may find in the drives I have attempted to describe, a memory of happy hours.

PERSIS F. CHASE.

LANCASTER, N. H., 1887.

CONTENTS.

8 *Contents.*

✿ The ✿ Lancaster Sketch Book.

"THE DAYS OF AULD LANG SYNE."

IN 1825, the village of Lancaster contained 34 houses, most of them cheaply built, and unpainted. There were two taverns. The stage tavern at the north end of the village, kept by William Cargill, standing where Jacob Benton's house now does. This building was moved a little farther north, and is now occupied as a tenement house. The other was the American House kept by Samuel White. This building was partly destroyed by fire, and has lately been taken down.

There was only one church in the village, a large, unfinished building, standing on sand hill, about where the meeting-house common is now. The hill at that time was very steep. A number of wooden steps led up to the meeting-house. I do not think our village forefathers were very wise in choosing such an elevated position, for on a summer's day the view from the door must have been so beautiful that I am sure some were tempted " to be doorkeepers in the house of the Lord " instead of going inside. Parson Willard preached in the meeting-house for many years at a salary of $150 a year.

This building was erected in 1791, when there were only 26 voters in town. In 1846 the old meeting-house was moved down the hill, to the spot where it now stands, and has since been known as the town hall.

There was a Methodist society who held services in the court house, which stood where Kimball Fletcher's house now does. The room was warmed by a potash kettle inverted on a brick arch.

Some prominent lawyers attended court here about the time I am writing of,—Daniel Webster, Levi Woodbury, Ichabod Bartlett, Joseph Bell, among the number.

Gen. John Wilson was clerk of the Common Pleas Court, of which Arthur Livermore was chief justice. Adino N. Brackett was clerk of the Superior Court, William M. Richardson, chief justice. Major John W. Weeks was sheriff.

The jail stood where the present one does. It was built of heavy hewed timbers of elm. It was used for 53 years, being burnt in 1858.

A little red gun house stood where the Unitarian church now does, where a brass cannon was kept, used by the artillery company. The postoffice was kept in the south-west room in the Fletcher house. Samuel A. Pearson, who then occupied the house, was postmaster. The mail south went out twice a week, carried in a two-horse wagon, and was three days in reaching Boston, stopping at Haverhill the first, and Concord the second night. The mail was carried to Colebrook once a week, to Bethel once a week on the way to Portland, by a man on horseback.

The physicians were Benjamin Hunking, Eliphalet Lyman and Jacob Stickney, who went their rounds on horseback, with the saddlebag containing their medicine swung across the horse's back.

There were four stores. One kept by Perkins, Eastman & Co., a building that was situated where Irving Drew's house is now. Another kept by Benjamin Boardman, in what is now known as the Rix house. The other two were at the south end of the village, and kept by Samuel White and Reuben Stephenson.

The stock of goods kept was very small, the sale of liquors making an important part of the trade. There was no law to prevent or regulate the selling of liquor. New England rum was considered essential during haying and harvesting. Cider was made in large quantities and used freely in all farmer's families. Ready-made clothing was unknown, as well as the modern machine-made hosiery for underwear. The wool and flax which every farmer raised, was spun and woven into cloth by the busy housewife and her daughters. A tailoress went from house to house making this cloth into garments for the men and boys.

Women, for ordinary wear, used home-made cloth, spun and woven by themselves. Flannel for winter and linen fabrics for summer. Dresses were made very plain, six to seven yards of cloth, three-fourths wide, was considered a large pattern.

Every fall the shoemaker went with his bench and tools to each house, when a corner of the kitchen was given up to him until the family were all shod. The shoemakers were Samuel Humux, an old Englishman from London, Heber Blanchard and Josiah Smith.

There was no wheelwright or competent painter in the place. Judge Lovejoy and Richard Eastman were house carpenters. Ephraim Cross manufactured hats in a small way. Allen Smith was saddler and harness maker. Warren Porter had a black-smith shop opposite his house which is now occupied by his son.

There was a grist mill and saw mill at the Wesson place, the miller, Squire Darby. Another grist mill stood where the present one does, Mr. Greenleaf, an old, white-headed revolutionary veteran, being miller.

There was a clothing mill and carding works where the Freeman mill is now.

The wages of laboring men was fifty cents a day and board, house carpenters and most mechanics commanded one dollar a day and board. The tailoress and dressmaker considered twenty-five cents a day ample remuneration for their work. Seventy-five cents a week was all the most competent housemaid received.

Only a few remain to tell us of the old days. Nearly all have gone " the way of all the world."

Fifty years have brought great changes, not only to this village, but to all New England. The rail-road, telegraph and telephone, and innumerable inventions to facilitate labor, have been invented within that time.

Progression is seen on every hand- the old making way for the new--which is as it should be.

" Let the great world spin forever down the ringing grooves of change."

EMMONS STOCKWELL.

Emmons Stockwell, the subject of this sketch,
was born in Petersham, Mass. As he was bereft of
his parents at an early age, he was bound out to
service during his minority. In order to encourage
enlistments, a regulation was made that indentured
apprentices should be entitled to their freedom if
they would enlist in the public service. Stockwell,
although very young, took advantage of this provision which gave him his liberty. He was in one
of the expeditions which went up for the invasion
of Canada during the French war. On returning
from this expedition he, with some others, came
down the Connecticut River, and for the first time
beheld this magnificent valley. A few years later,
remembering the great natural attractions, he decided to return and make his home here.

His glowing account of the Connecticut valley
interested others, and in the spring of 1764, he
started with Captain David Page, David Page, Jr.,

and a few others from Petersham, to seek their
fortunes in Northern New Hampshire. The whole
country was then a dense wilderness; not a highway had been constructed in or to our town.

The early settlers found their way by marked
trees through the woods. They drove before them
some twenty head of cattle, with bags of salt, pro-
visions and farming tools fastened to their horns.
They erected their first camp on what is now known
as Holton meadow, and went immediately at work
to clear some land. In a short time they had twelve
acres planted with corn. It grew so rapidly that by
the 25th of August it was twelve feet high, and in
full milk, but this fair prospect of a good crop of
corn was entirely destroyed by a hard frost that
came on the 26th; but perseverance was the motto
of our forefathers. They managed to keep their
cattle through the winter by cutting the grass on
the open land on Beaver Brook, and were ready to
renew the struggles of another year.

The nearest mill was a No. 4, in the town of
Charlestown; but the settlers did not depend upon
food transported from there for their daily use.
Emmons Stockwell made a huge mortar which held
two bushels. Into this, corn, beans, and rye
were put, and pounded with a great wooden

pestle. Cooked potatoes and vegetables were mixed with the contents of the mortar and the whole was baked together. This composition was called " thump," and was considered a delicious dish, so I am told.

The first white woman that came to Lancaster was Ruth Page. Her father, Governor Page, so called by way of distinction merely, never resided in Lancaster, but was a sort of director of the settlement, making frequent journeys to visit the new colony, and by his counsel rendered them great aid in the management of their affairs. Captain David Page and son, who were among the first who came here, were his brother and nephew.

In August, 1764, Governor Page started from Petersham on horseback, accompanied by Ruth, who was going to Lancaster to cook the food and do the work for the little colony, then more than forty miles from their nearest neighbors.

On the 25th of August, the night of the great frost, Governor Page and his daughter slept in the woods in Orford. They arrived in Lancaster the last of the month to find the little colony somewhat disheartened by the great calamity that had befallen them, but were no doubt much cheered to know a woman had come to make their homes more comfortable.

Ruth must have had a rather nice time, notwith-standing the rough life. There were no other girls to share the attention of the young men, and when Emmons began to pay attention to her, as he soon did, she had no one to be jealous of.

The next year after Ruth's arrival in Lancaster, she was married to Emmons Stockwell, and began housekeeping on the old Stockwell place. A part of the old house is now standing. She was, at the time of her marriage, eighteen years old, and he was twenty-three. Mrs. Stockwell was a woman of great determination of character. She had won-derful general capacity; she could do anything that was necessary, and did everything well. It is said that in the days of the Revolution she was the sal-vation of the colony. The hardships and dangers which surrounded them, the capture of the settlers by the Indians, and gloomy prospects of the country, somewhat weakened the resolutions of the settlers. They met at Mr. Stockwell's house to discuss the abandonment of the town. Mrs. Stockwell declared that she would not go away; that she knew no such thing as failure. Others were influenced by the decision of the Stockwells, and the settlement was saved.

Mr. Stockwell had a vigorous mind, a great deal of good common sense, and possessed prodigous strength. He could neither read nor write, until taught by his wife. For many years there was no school or school house. Mrs. Stockwell, who was a very good scholar for those early days, taught the children of the settlement in her own house. The next year after Mrs. Stockwell's marriage, Edward Bucknam, one of the young settlers, married a sister of Mrs. Stockwell, who had probably come to make her sister a visit. They settled at the mouth of Beaver Brook, a stream that runs through Martin meadows. A hunter who caught a large number of beavers, which abounded in this stream, gave his name to the meadows. The Bucknams had six children, from whom have descended the Moores, McIntires, Howes and Bucknams. Their oldest daughter, Eunice, was the first child born in the settlement. It was a long time before any traveled public way was constructed. Canoes were the only carriages, and they were made by themselves from the trunks of great trees. The women could row these canoes up and down the river with great skill; and could also handle the rifle and fishing pole with expertness. As the rivers and streams were full of fish, and the forest of moose and other game, the tables of our ancestors must have been supplied with something besides " thump."

Mr. and Mrs. Stockwell lived together more than fifty-five years, and had fifteen children, seven sons and eight daughters, all of whom grew to maturity. Before Mrs. Stockwell's death she could number one hundred and ninety living descendants. She died at the age of eighty-two; her husband at seventy-eight. David Stockwell, their oldest child, was the first son of Lancaster.

Edward Bucknam, whom I have mentioned before, was a very useful man to the new colony. He was a good surveyor, and could " draw teeth " and " let blood," and perform the marriage service. He laid out a large portion of the town and many of the highways.

The first bridge erected in town was the old " Stockwell bridge," across Israel's River. The right to cross it first was put up at auction, and bid off by Emmons Stockwell, for five gallons of brandy which cost him forty-two shillings a gallon.

The prosperity and success of our town is, no doubt, owing in a great measure to the fact that its foundations were laid by such men as Stockwell and Bucknam, and honor and gratitude should be given to the memory of Ruth Stockwell, who came through the wilderness to aid the new settlers, and who, by perseverance and courage, overcame all obstacles and lived to see the " wilderness blossom like the rose."

THE DRIVE TO STOCKWELL FARM.

In going to the Stockwell farm and through the pine woods to the Northumberland road, we drive to the north end of the village, and take the road to the right, which is bordered on either side with tidy, home-like looking houses, the yards in front bright with flowers, and far away to the right and left are charming mountain views. After crossing the rail-road track, we turn to the left, which takes us directly to the Stockwell farm, the highway ending there. We pass on the right the Abbott place, and what was formerly known as the Barton G. Towne farm. These farms were originally settled by the Pages.

Adjoining this is the Stockwell farm, which extends to the bank of the Connecticut river. The first land cleared in Lancaster was twelve acres of this farm near the river, by Emmons Stockwell, in

April, 1764, and planted with corn. The broad intervale that stretches away in undulating swells to the river, has been known for a hundred and twenty years as the " Stockwell Farm," and occupied since the death of Emmons Stockwell, by his descendants.

Driving on, we pass a beautiful grove of elms, and just below stands the Stockwell farm -house. The low, moss covered ell connected with it is the first frame building erected in Lancaster, and was the home for many years of Ruth Stockwell, the first white woman that came to this town.

To the right of the buildings, which stand upon a slight elevation, we look down upon a grand and extensive meadow view. The river at this point makes a sweeping curve toward Vermont, leaving an expanse of three hundred acres of green intervale on the New Hampshire side. A most charming background for this green valley is first formed by the Connecticut river and beyond that the hills of Vermont. Nearly in front of us, rising in symetrical beauty, are Mt. McClellan and Mt. Rogers, whose tree crowned sides descend into undulating farms. Driving down the bank, we go on through the meadow, passing fields of nodding rye and oats, to the river, whose banks are gracefully fringed with trees. Turning again, we drive up the bank, passing through some bars on the left, and drive across a level field. We are now on the old road to Northumberland, but long since it ceased to be a highway. On our right we pass the agricultural fair grounds, beyond is the Pilot range, flecked with shadows, and still farther on rise the familiar outlines of the White Mountains. We soon enter the woods. Is it not delightful? Take long breaths of the fragrant, spicy air, for " our pines are trees of healing."

Listen to the sighing breath of the trees. Henry Ward Beecher says, " the first pines must have grown on the sea shore, and learned their first accents from the surf and the waves; and all their posterity have inherited the sound, and borne it inland to the mountains."

The friendly boughs seem to nod welcome to us. On either side is a wild tangle of ferns, dog wood and elder blooms, while our carriage wheels roll over a carpet of pine needles. All too soon we emerge into the sunshine, and turning to the right find ourselves in the highway, homeward bound.

The road we are now on was formerly the stage route to Groveton. We drive into the village by

Summer St., getting a fine view of Mt. Prospect; the road winding in a zig-zag course up its side, is distinctly seen from this point. We soon finish our drive, but the memory of broad meadows, mountain peaks and lovely pine woods, will remain with us.

Surely the variety and beauty of the drives in this vicinity cannot be surpassed; whichever way one goes "they cannot err in this delightful region."

MAJOR JONAS WILDER.

The first framed dwelling house erected in Lancaster was the large, square, flat-roofed building, that stands at the north end of the village, known as the "Holton house."

This house was considered at the time it was built a very elegant residence; the finest in the county. It was built by Major Jonas Wilder, who was born in Lyme, Conn., on the 22d of February, 1732. When quite young he went to Templeton, Mass. where he resided many years. In the course of time, reports came to Major Wilder of the rich land that had been discovered in the valley of the Connecticut in Upper Coos. He determined to go and explore the region, which he did. On reaching Lancaster, he was delighted with the natural loveliness of this valley. In imagination he saw the broad meadows, which at that time were covered with trees, cleared and planted with corn, the river gleaming like a band of silver through the fresh verdure, while the encircling chain of mountains, seemed a fitting frame for so fair a picture.

Major Wilder decided to go no farther, but bought a mile square of land extending from the " Holton house " to Israel's river.

He then returned to Templeton, to make arrangements to remove to Lancaster, and take possession of his new estate.

In Feb., 1780, he started from Templeton with his wife and ten children, and a train consisting of two family sleighs, four lumber sleighs and a number of sleds for stores. He also brought along carpenters, masons and glaziers, and everything for building purposes.

I do not know how long they were in reaching Lancaster, but probably some weeks. A small house was built for a temporary home, near the river bank,—remains of this building can still be seen on the Holton meadow—and some land cleared and planted with corn. On the 19th of May, 1780, memorable as the " dark day," they commenced digging the cellar for the great house, but by eleven o'clock it became so dark that the men were obliged to discontinue the work.

This strange and as yet unexplained phenomenon of nature, extended throughout New England, and created great disturbance in the minds of the people, and caused much commotion among the animal creation. The fowls went to roost, the birds suddenly stopped their blithesome singing and disappeared, the cattle returned to their stalls, lowing pitifully. Candles were lighted in the houses, and everything bore the aspect of the darkest night.

Many were convinced that the end of the world had come, and betook themselves to devotions.

All worldly things have long since come to an end for those who witnessed the " dark day," but the sun has shone on with undiminished splendor through the cycles of the years.

The frame of this house was raised on the 26th of July, 1780. I have not been able to ascertain the exact date of the completion of the building.

As there was no church built until the year 1794, religious services were held at this house, also the town meetings. In 1780, Major Wilder was chosen on a committee to select a public burying ground, he presented the mound known as the "old burying ground," to the town to be used for that purpose. The first grist and saw mill in town were built by Major Wilder. He also assisted in laying out roads. He cleared a large tract of meadow land, where he raised five hundred bushels of corn. I have been told that this land was so rich, that for years no dressing was necessary, and what would now be considered of great value was thrown in the Connecticut.

The county was thickly settled with Indians at the time Major Wilder came here. He was noted for his hospitable and humane care for them, and was rewarded by their faithful friendship.

He was a valuable accession to the new settlement, and has left a record of which his descendants may well be proud.

Of his numerous family, only one great-grandchild is living in town at the present time.

He died in 1810 of paralysis. A handsome granite monument recently constructed by a great grandson, Mr. C. O. Baker of Portland, Me., marks the spot in the old cemetery where his ashes repose.

THE DRIVE TO JEFFERSON.

The White Mountain region is especially delightful, affording as it does from almost any point, charming and picturesque drives.

The situation of Lancaster is particularly favored in this respect. In any direction you may go,

> " Aloft on sky and mountain wall,
> Are God's great pictures hung."

Perhaps the drive to Jefferson, going over the " Jefferson Mills Road," and returning by the " north road," affords as grand a view of the White and Franconia ranges as can be had in this vicinity.

We go up the sand hill and leave the village by Portland St. On our right is Holton hill, a splendid situation for a summer hotel. The road is ascending most of the way for the next mile, which brings us to the top of " LeGro hill." Before we begin the descent, let us stop and enjoy the beautiful views. To the right of us, to the left of us, and in front of us, the horizon is terraced with mountains. The cultivated uplands in the foreground, are golden in the afternoon sunshine. On our left is the Pilot range, broken by cones and peaks, while the soft clouds that fleck the sky, are painting the mountain sides with shadows of every imaginable form and shape. Nearly in front, the whole White Mountain range stands massive and majestic, the pride of New Hampshire, as it has stood for thousands of years. The gorges and ravines that channel the sides of the mountains can be plainly seen. To the right, the irregular peaks of the Franconia range are distinctly outlined against the blue sky. Who can behold this mighty chain of mountains at a fitting hour in the afternoon, and fail to be impressed with the view? The grandeur of it cannot be over estimated.

We go on down the hill, past as good' farming land as there is in town, but the stone walls that surround some portion of it are a good evidence that the soil has been redeemed from rocks and stones, smoothed and enriched by indomitable industry. Driving briskly along, passing some pleasant and comfortable looking homes, we arrive at the " Mills," once a lively little business place, but now reminding one of the " deserted village." We take the road to the left, cross a rickety bridge and are on the direct route to " Jefferson Hill," a pleasant shady road, with some quite steep hills. We soon pass a beautiful maple grove. The underbrush has been removed, and seats arranged beneath the dense foliage of the trees, affording a delightful place for picnics and gatherings. By the look of some of the land we pass, the stories of sheep having· their noses sharpened to get at the grass between the stones, can be easily believed.

Presently we come in sight of the village of " Jefferson Hill," and can distinguish the " Waumbek " house quite distinctly. As we are not going to visit the village, we will take the turn to the left and are on the North road, and soon come to an entire change of scenery. The road is no longer hilly, and quite a broad sweep of level land borders it on either side, the hills that lie beyond are thickly covered with trees. In the Autumn this is an especially delightful drive, then these hillsides are one mass of gorgeous coloring.

A little further on, a stream of water comes rushing down the hillside, through a green pasture, where a flock of geese are giving lessons to their young in aquatic sports, but at our approach stretch their necks and hiss, evidently taking us for enemies. Some humane persons have placed a wooden trough at the roadside, and into this the water comes in a sparkling stream, into which our horse is anxious to plunge his nose. How he seems to enjoy it, drinking so heartily. Then he lifts his head and takes a look down the road, to see who is coming. Some work horses turned loose in an adjacent field, affecting gayety in their old age, attract his attention, but we remind him he has other business to attend to. Another mile brings us to a point where the road diverges to the right and left. The one to the right leading to Gore, and Groveton, the left is our way home, so we turn that way.

Bray Hill, on the edge of Whitefield, presently comes into view, and although not much of an elevation, is so situated that both the White and Franconia ranges can be seen at good advantage from the summit.

We are now approaching the part of the town known as " out east," where some of the most desirable farms in Lancaster are situated. The houses are comfortable, and some quite handsome, with neat and tastefully kept yards and commodious barns, which indicate that prosperity has attended the efforts of the laborer.

The " great brook " crosses and winds itself through the green fields on its way to Israel's river. The sun is just sinking behind the Vermont hills, tinging with a rosy light the Pilot Range and Per-

cy Peaks. How beautiful it is! but already the
shadows are creeping down the mountain sides, reminding us that we must hasten home, and presently we find ourselves at our own door, bringing with
us pictures of mountains, hills, forest and field, that
will live in our memory forever.

THE BUILDING OF THE FIRST CHURCH
IN LANCASTER.

It was a number of years after the first settlers
had found their way to this pleasant valley, and had,
by such hardships as only the pioneers in a new
country can experience, made for themselves homes
by the fertile banks of the Connecticut, and on the
rugged hill-sides, before they could raise the means
to build a church.

Religious services had been held in private
houses, and after Major Wilder's handsome man-
sion was completed, it answered well for that purpose. In the year 1791, the question of building a
" meeting-house," was considered at the town
meeting. A committee of six was appointed to
buy six acres on the plain above the sand hill, and

inspect the clearing of the same, " for a meeting-house plot."

Later, a committee was chosen " to propose a plan for the meeting-house." After due consideration the following was recommended: " That the pews be sold at public auction. That each person give his note to the committee, who shall be authorized to receive the pay and appropriate the same. That each person be subjected to the following method of payment: --That the whole sum be divided into four parts, to be paid the four next succeeding years. That each person pay six shillings and eight pence on the pound the first year, one half in June, the other in November, the rest to be divided into three equal parts, and paid in November of each year. That four shillings on the pound, be paid in cash, or salts of lye, and the rest in wheat at four shillings per bushel, or beef at seventeen shillings and six pence per hundred weight, with this restriction, that the committee shall receive each man's equal proportion of timber, boards, clapboards and shingles, if good and merchantable. That each person who buys a pew, shall procure sufficient bonds for payment, and his obligation shall be lodged in the hands of the chairman of the committee, which shall be taken up or endorsed by a receipt from the committee."

These conditions were accepted by the people, and the following men were chosen " to build the meeting-house: " Col. Jonas Wilder, Capt. John Weeks, Lieut. Emmons Stockwell, Lieut. Joseph Brackett, Lieut. Dennis Stanley and Capt. David Page.

It was nearly four years before the church was finished. From the " old Town Hall building," which is the old " meeting-house," one would not suppose it to have been a very imposing edifice, but such it is said to have been. Certainly it was a prominent feature in the landscape, standing on the brow of the hill, which at that time was very steep, like some grim sentinel keeping watch of the little hamlet that clustered in the valley below. It was built with a steeple at one end, two porches, and a broad entrance on the side. There was a gallery, a high pulpit, with a sounding-board suspended above. The pews were square, and the seats arranged so they could be raised up when the congregation stood up for prayers, making more room. When the minister said Amen, the clapping of the falling seats made a great clatter. A long flight of steps led up to the entrance for the accommodation of those who went on foot, and horse-blocks were provided for the mounting and dismounting of those who came on horse-back.

There was no provision made at all for warming the church. Some of the women carried foot stoves, an arrangement of sheet iron in a wooden frame in which coals could be put.

In 1794, the question of settling a minister was considered at the town meeting, and a committee of nine persons was selected to " draw proposals for the settlement and salary of the Rev. Joseph Willard."

At the next town meeting the following report was made: " To give Rev. Joseph Willard fifty pounds a year for the next succeeding three years. This was to increase as the inventory of the town increased, till it reached eighty pounds. To be paid on the first day of March of each year. One third part paid in cash, the other two thirds in produce. On condition that we can get help from the neighboring towns as we now expect."

It was ascertained that the town of Northumberland would pay ten pounds toward the salary of Mr. Willard, on condition that he would preach a proportion of the time at that place. At the same town meeting that the arrangement in regard to hiring the minister was made, it was voted " to raise twenty-six dollars to be laid out in smoothing the meeting-house plot." It was voted to pay three shillings and six pence per day, "if they found their board and tools."

On the 18th of September, 1794, Rev. Joseph Willard was installed as pastor over a church of twenty-four persons, and continued to occupy this position for twenty-eight years.

Those who remember this gentleman, speak of him in the highest terms of respect. His religious teachings were full of charity and love, and left an abiding influence for good.

I am told that he was very stately and dignified, with something of a military air which he had acquired in the army, and a thorough gentleman of the old school. He continued during his life to adhere to the fashion of knee-breeches, shoes with silver buckles, and carried a cane.

" He was a man to all the country dear
And passing rich with fifty pounds a year.
Remote from towns he ran his godly race.
Nor e're had changed, nor wished to change his place;
But in his duty prompt at every call,
He watched and wept, he prayed and felt for all.
He tried each art, reproved each dull delay,
Allured to brighter worlds, and led the way."

The following are the names of the ministers that have been settled by the Congregational Society since its commencement, as far as I have been able to ascertain:

Joseph Willard,	Andrew Govan,
Luke Spofford,	—— Buxton,
Clark Perry,	David Perry,
Stephen A. Barnard,	Isaac Weston,
E. B. Chamberlain,	Prescott Fay,
Henry V. Emmons,	C. E. Harrington,
C. E. Sumner,	S. A. Burnaby.
Jason R. Wheelock,	

The names of the deacons were:

Jonas Baker,	Samuel Phelps,
Joseph Wilder,	Reuben W. Freeman,
Elias Chapman,	Porter Freeman,
William Farrar,	Edward C. Spaulding,
Seth Adams,	Azro Burton.
William Freeman,	

In 1839, the church that is now occupied by the Congregational Society was built. The good and true men who founded this church among the wilds of New Hampshire, have all passed on to " another country," but the church and society have continued to increase in power and numbers, as the years have passed, and many

" Seek by the path which their fore-fathers trod
Through the land of their sojourn—the kingdom of God."

THE DRIVE TO NORTHUMBERLAND.
RETURNING ON THE VERMONT SIDE OF THE CONNECTICUT RIVER.

Some pleasant afternoon in June, when grass and trees are wearing their first freshness of summer, what can be more enjoyable than a drive to Northumberland Falls, returning by way of the Vermont side of the Connecticut river?

We drive to the North end of Main street, and take the road to the right. Passing the jail, we soon see on our left Baker Pond, once a famous place for pickerel. A little further on, a curve in the road affords us a charming meadow view. Some of these acres of broad intervale that roll away in waves of " living green " to the banks of the Connecticut, belong to the Stockwell farm. We go on past the Fair ground and " the old Bellows place," and soon enter the cool and fragrant pine woods, where only a glimpse of the blue sky is seen above the rustling tree tops. These woods that seem so delightful on a summer afternoon, was the place where once a robbery was attempted. Mr. Hartwell, a gentleman who formerly resided in Lancaster, owned a very fine horse remarkable for speed. One very dark night, he was driving down to L., when about half through the pine woods, a man sprang from the road-side, caught the horse by the bridle, and presenting a pistol, commanded him to stop. Mr. H. struck the horse a hard blow, he gave a tremendous jump, threw the man down and was off like an arrow, far beyond the reach of the robber, before he had regained his feet.

A very eccentric man by the name of Ziba Lines once had a home under these pine woods, where he lived many years a hermit's life. I am informed his seclusion from the world was caused by a disappointment in love.

As we go on, we notice on our right, masses of granite rocks, flung up in vast ledges, their sides mossed over, and from the rifts and clefts, bushes and dwarfed hemlocks are growing. Now we pass on our left, acres of level meadow land. In some places the green turf has been turned over, and we conclude from the number of thieving crows, flying near, that corn has been planted there.

In the distance, but seemingly directly in front of us, are to be seen the twin mountains, known as the " Percy Peaks," whose cone-like tops are conspicuous from almost every point of view. Now we are approaching the little village known as The Falls.

We hear the hum of the mills along the river side, and see great piles of newly sawed lumber, that perfumes the air with a piney smell.

Crossing the long covered bridge, we are in Guildhall, Vt., a small, but pleasantly located village. We drive through the principal street, noticing the comfortable and home-like looking houses. The two churches stand sociably side by side. Another mile brings us to a turn in the road, where a charming view can be had. On our left we can see a long distance down the river

" Not unknown to classic song,
Which still in varying beauty rolls along."

Not a ripple disturbs the surface of the water, that with mirror-like exactness reflects the trees, that so gracefully fringe its banks. On the right, the rolling hills that further on swell into rugged mountains. On we go with the river on our left all the way. In some places the trees are so large along the bank, that we get only a glimpse of the blue water. Birds are singing blithely, as they flit from tree to tree. The red squirrel runs along the fence. Graceful, feather-like ferns are growing in great clusters in the more shaded places. Now, we are coming to the Ames place. Where can a finer meadow view than this be seen? The river takes a wide circuit toward New Hampshire, leaving a grand expanse of intervale, dotted thickly with the graceful meadow elm. Beyond the gleaming of the river, Pilot Range perfects the artistic finish of the picture. From this point until the toll bridge is reached, a fine combination of river and mountain scenery is presented. Those who think

> " 'Tis distance lends enchantment to the view,
> And robes the mountain in its azure hue,"

will enjoy the drive. Crossing the bridge, we are in the Granite State again, and as the

> " Evening shadows are displayed,
> Evening damps begin to fall,"

arrive at our home, delighted with our drive of twelve miles.

ZIBA LINES.

Doubtless there are many in town who remember Ziba Lines, who had a small house situated near the place where the house now occupied by Captain Beattie is standing.

Mr. Lines came to this town from Charlestown, N. H. He had been at work for a number of years for a wealthy man in that place, and brought quite a sum of money here with him. When he first came to Lancaster he was fond of society, and used to go to places of amusement, and as he had considerable musical ability, was quite noted for singing songs.

Probably all would have gone on prosperously with Ziba, had he not fallen in love, which, alas! was not reciprocated; the lady would not listen to his suit, and he was unable to say, " Nay, if she loves me not, I care not for her," but brooded over his disappointment until he became a hermit and a miser.

He bought a number of acres of land, in what is known as the pine woods, built a house which I have mentioned, where he lived isolated from every one. After a few years he became so eccentric that he was considered almost insane, but perfectly harmless and quiet.

At one time he invited a number of people to attend his wedding, requesting the minister to go to the home of the lady at a certain time, to perform the marriage ceremony. He then went to his lady love, whom he found milking, and told her what he had done. For a reply, she threw the milk, pail and all, at poor Ziba, and ran away. I don't know how the milk bath affected him, but probably it had

a quieting affect, as after that he turned his attention
more to money. He got all he had exchanged into
silver, and kept it in two brown earthen pots, that
held about a gallon a piece, and these he usually kept
buried in the ground.

One Sunday the people in the church were surprised by seeing Mr. Lines walk up the aisle, with
these pots, one under each arm. He deposited them
on the table under the pulpit, and remained standing
near until the service was over. When he was
asked what he had brought the money to church for,
he replied that he " had made an offering of it to the
Lord," and when some one offered to take care of it,
he decided to do so himself. He then carried the
pots of money to Mr. Bellows, who lived in the
house known as "the old Bellows house." A colored
woman was living in the family at that time. She
got an empty trunk, and in this Mr. Lines deposited
his treasures, taking the key away with him. Some
time after, the trunk was opened, and found to contain only stones. No one knew when he had taken
the money away, but it was ascertained that he
went one night, carried it away, and buried it some-
where in the pine woods, where it is supposed to remain until this day.

Mr. Lines had some trouble with a neighbor about

a line fence. This man would build a stump fence that would require two yoke of oxen and two men all day to place in position.

During the night, Mr. Lines would entirely remove it with the help of only one small yoke of steers.

An immense chain, weighing two hundred pounds, was used by his neighbor in moving the stumps. One night this chain disappeared, but a track across a plowed field to the river bank, indicated it had been drawn across and thrown into the river. The river was dragged, but the chain was never found.

A few years ago, Emmons Stockwell plowed this chain up, when he was breaking up some land. Mr. Lines had buried it as he did his money.

As Mr. Lines became old, it was not considered safe for him to live alone. There was a guardian appointed for him, and he was removed to Page Hill, where he died a victim of unrequited love.

THF DRIVE TO SOUTH LANCASTER

The drive to South Lancaster, returning by way of the Vermont side of the Connecticut river, affords some of the most beautiful meadow views in this vicinity.

> " The tasseled maize, full grain or clover,
>   Far o'er the level meadow grows,
>   And through it, like a wayward rover,
>   The noble river gently flows."

We go up Baker hill, and after passing several cottages, come to the two story white house, situated on a hill at the left. This house is now occupied by W. H. Hanson, but was built by Parson Willard, and known for many years as the parsonage. A little further on, standing on a hill remote from any building, we notice the little brick powder house, formerly owned by the State, and the powder for the guns that used to be stored in the old arsenal, on the opposite side of the road, was kept there, but since the old militia system was abolished, the arsenal has been made into a stable, and the powder house sold to R. P. Kent, Son & Co., who used it for storing powder. We drive along what used to be the old stage road to Littleton. Ah! how well we remember those morning rides, long before daylight, in the lumbering old stage coach, with Jim Pool for a driver. Surely it is a good thing that the world moves, that the march of improvement has rendered that twenty mile drive to reach the cars, unnecessary. We pass neat, home-like looking farm houses. On the right are the broad meadows, and just beyond the silvery gleaming of the river, are the cultivated lands, farm houses and hills of Vermont, making up an ideal landscape view of intervale, river and mountain.

Presently we come to the Brackett hill, and see on our left, the old brick house cosily situated at the foot of it, with broad, spreading butternut trees at one side. We pass the bridge over the brook, that winds in and out with many a curve, through the pasture on the left, and a little farther on, we come to the old flat-roofed house, shaded by elms, formerly the home of Major John W. Weeks, one of the first settlers of Lancaster. Major Weeks won his military title at the battle of Chippewa, being promoted from Captain to the rank of Major for gallant conduct at that time. The road is smooth and level, we drive briskly along, getting a glimpse of the " shining river " through the dense foliage of the trees, pass the little brick school-house, and soon come to the " White farm." From the peculiar curve the river takes at this point, this farm has always been called the Catbow.

Soon after the revolutionary war, Major Moses White, of Rutland, Mass., was rewarded for the

honor and ability with which he had filled the high
position in the continental army, to which he had
been called, by receiving from the government,
through General Hazen, this tract of land where he
fixed his residence, and passed the remainder of his
life, leaving the farm to his descendants at his death,
by whom it was occupied for many years. On we
go over this pleasant river road, passing farm houses,
and acres of meadow land on the right, pastures
and cultivated fields on the left, with now and then
patches of woodland, until we come in sight of a
railway station, and a few other buildings at South
Lancaster.

Turning to the right, we cross the railroad track,
and the covered bridge that spans the Connecticut,
and are in Vermont. The views along the homeward drive are unsurpassed. From the brick house,
now known as the "Rowell place," formerly owned
by Reuben Benton, to the "Stone farm," a distance
of about one mile, the scenery is more picturesque
than at any other point during the drive. Here,
for a long distance the Connecticut is seen winding
in graceful curves through the broad intervales.
The varied tints of green displayed in grass, grain
and foliage, all bathed in the golden sunlight of a
summer afternoon, make a picture that must be

seen to be appreciated. On we go over the pleasant country road, sometimes through bits of woods, full of hemlock, pine, and spruce, that perfume the air with a spicy odor, then out into the sunshine, where we see the regal golden rod waving its plumy head among the raspberry and blackberry bushes at the roadside. In some places the purple aster is beginning to fringe the way, and the wild clematis to trail its graceful vines over the fences. A golden robin is perched on the swaying limb of a tree in front of us, singing a merry song, and the meadow lark skims over the green fields rejoicing as he flies.

Now we are passing the " Clark farm," owned by Deacon Carlton, and presently the " old Hopkins place " comes into view, now the property of the Rhodes Brothers, two fine specimens of Connecticut river farms. A charming back ground for these broad meadows, is formed by the rich rolls of cultivated land, on " Stebbins hill," and other hills that have no name. Flashes of sunlight turn acres of woods on Mt. Prospect and Mt. Pleasant into patches of shining satin. The White mountains, Pilot Range and Percy Peaks, that now seem almost in front of us, are bathed in glorious sunset hues, of rose gold and purple; but we are approaching the old toll bridge, and are reminded that it is almost supper time, and as the old farmer wisely remarked, "folks can't live on scenery," we rapidly finish our delightful drive.

RICHARD C. EVERETT.

In November, 1787, a little party of emigrants might have been seen slowly wending their way through the woods toward Upper Coos.

There were only four persons, two men and one woman, and a little child, which the younger of the men, who was about eighteen, carried in his arms. The other man led a horse upon whose back was fastened a heavy load, and upon his own back was a pack.

The names of these persons were Mr. and Mrs. Blake and child, the young man was Richard C. Everett, who afterward became the first lawyer of Lancaster. As Richard had but little of his own to carry, the baby become his burden instead of its mother's.

On the 19th of October of the same year, Richard had been discharged from service in the revolutionary war at Yorktown among many others whose services were no longer needed.

Being an orphan and almost without friends, he had enlisted two years previous, when only sixteen years of age. During the first year he saw much hardship and privation. The short allowance of food, poor clothing and hard work, soon changed the robust and healthy boy so much, that even his mother, had she been alive, would hardly have known him. One day he was sent to General Washington's headquarters on some errand. The youthful appearance and sad condition of the poor boy attracted the General's sympathy. He enquired who he was and why he was there. After hearing his story, he was so kind as to take him into his personal service, where his duties were much lighter. After leaving the army he returned to Providence, his native place, and being entirely dependent upon his own exertions for a living, was looking about for some employment, when a proposition was made him by Mr. Blake, with whom he was acquainted, to go with him to Upper Coos, where it was reported that good land was cheap, and emigrants were wanted.

This Richard decided to do, and the little party started on their long tramp to seek their fortune in the wilds of Upper Coos.

Weary and foot-sore, this little band were overjoyed when just at night-fall on the twelfth day of their long march, they saw from a slight eminence they had reached, the smoke rising from some log houses in the valley beneath them, and knew they had at last arrived at Lancaster, their destination.

They had been directed to go to Major Wilder, who promised to be a kind of father to the new settlers. He gave them a hospitable welcome, and as he had been wanting to get some men to draw salt from Portland, before many days, Mr. Blake and Richard had agreed to work for him during the winter.

Before they could commence their labors, however, a road had to be made through the Notch sufficiently wide for a sled to pass through. The road at that time being hardly more than a foot path. This was done by Mr. Blake and Richard, assisted by one other man.

During the winter Richard saved all he could of his earnings, as he had made up his mind he would have an education. Perhaps Persis, daughter of Major Wilder, whom he afterward married, inspired him to make this decision. In the spring he went to Hanover, where he managed by hard work and economy to prepare himself for college, and he determined to take a collegiate course, although his resources were limited to good health and willing hands. But, after all these years of hardship, the way was unexpectedly opened to him. One day in looking over a Boston paper, he saw an advertisement wanting information of the heirs of Richard Everett, formerly of Providence. Richard knew it must mean his father. He immediately wrote to the address given, and in reply was informed that he must go to Providence and prove that he was the son of Richard Everett, in which case quite a sum of money was ready to be paid to him.

This he did, having no difficulty in proving himself the rightful heir.

In surveying and laying out the city of Providence, it had been found that several lots of land belonged to Richard Everett. These had been sold to good advantage; so Richard found himself possessed of sufficient means to finish his education, and have something left.

After graduating, he studied law, and in 1793 returned to Lancaster, and began the practice of his profession. He was married to Persis Wilder, December 7, 1793, after an engagement of nine years.

They had seven children, all daughters, none of whom are now living.

Judge Everett built the house known as the "Cross place," where he resided until his death, which occurred on the 22nd of March, 1815.

He was successful as a lawyer, became judge of the Court of Common Pleas, and afterwards judge of the Supreme Court, which office he held for many years.

THE DRIVE TO STEBBINS HILL.

The view from Stebbins Hill is one of the most charming in this vicinity.

Driving up Baker Hill, and along the river road for a mile and a half, we come to a turn on our left, which we will take.

The road soon begins to be ascending, but smooth and hard. Presently we come to the "Emerson place." formerly owned by Captain John Weeks, who was the first to settle on this hill land.

Perhaps one reason for choosing this high land, was owing to the freshets that every spring delayed the cultivation of the intervales until frequently as late as June, and perhaps the exceedingly lovely view from this hill was the attraction.

On the right, a short distance above the "Emerson place," is the old McIntire farm, settled by John McIntire, who came to this town in 1794, married for his first wife Sally Stockwell, daughter of Emmons Stockwell, one of the first settlers of the town. Mr. McIntire was quite a remarkable man. He could neither read nor write, but invented a method of computing interest, and " dod sir," was his favorite expression, he always was correct in his calculations. He accumulated quite a large property, which he divided equally among his sixteen children before his death.

On we go still up, about a mile above the McIntire place the road turns to the left. On the right, just at the crown, but somewhat back, is the " Stebbins place," formerly owned by Edward Spaulding, who was the son of Phineas and Phebe Spaulding, who settled in the town of Northumberland, in the year 1769. Mrs. Spaulding was a descendant of the famous Mrs. Dustin and was a woman of great courage and determination. Edward Spaulding was brought in his mother's arms from Haverhill to Northumberland, through the wilderness, alone, with only spotted trees for a guide.

The road is getting pretty steep, but a few more rods brings to just the right point for the view. The scene is beautiful and picturesque, and one that will live in the memory forever.

The windings of the Connecticut can be traced many miles, through the broad, green, beautiful meadows, waving with grass, and grain and patches of glistening corn, reminding us that though among the beauties of nature, the hand of man has added something to its charms.

From east to west a mighty chain of mountains swells gracefully along the horizon. The most distant seem to touch the heavens and lose themselves amid the clouds.

Below us, cosily situated in the green valley, the houses of the village of L. gleam white in the afternoon sunshine.

A little more than a hundred years have passed along the course of time, since how changed was the scene!

The same river, hills and mountains were here, and will still stand unchanged, unchanging through ages yet to come. But yonder village, and the comfortable farm houses, surrounded by acres of cultivated land, where were they?

Lancaster was a wilderness, and Indian hunters strode along its hills and valleys. The wild deer lapped the water of the river that flowed sparkling through the meadows beneath us.

Where the village now stands, the smoke from a

few log cabins of the first settlers curled above the trees of the forest.

Who can reflect upon the changes that have already been, without turning the mind toward the future? Slowly we drive along, reluctant to leave this beautiful prospect, but

" The western waves of ebbing day,"

remind us that it is time we were on our way home. We go on, descending the hill on the opposite side from which we came, and soon turn into the Whitefield road, reaching the village by way of the Sand hill. We are sure that all who have seen this view from this hill at a fitting hour in the afternoon, and through a favoring air, will agree with the old gentleman who remarked to some city boarders, " I tell 'em if they want to see *scenyury*, Stebbins hill is the place."

PHEBE SPAULDING.

A great deal has been written in a general way, of the hardships endured by the first settlers of New England.

When we read of the Puritan Fathers landing on the " stern and rock-bound coast " of Massachusetts, and their trials and privations, we are filled with wonder and admiration at the courage and determination displayed by them, but occasionally there will come to us from the dim and distant past, traditions of courage and fortitude borne by our ancestors of a later day, that are equally as wonderful.

The following narrative, which is true, illustrates this in a forcible manner, and gives us some idea of what the women of that early day endured.

In the year 1769, a party of emigrants started from Londonderry, in the southern part of New Hampshire, for Upper Coos of the same state, the distance being about one hundred and fifty miles.

Glowing accounts had come to them of the fertile lands on the banks of the Connecticut that could be had for almost nothing, and inspired by the hope of winning a home and perhaps a fortune in this unbroken wilderness, they decided, notwithstanding the great hardships they would have to endure, to go.

Packing bedding and a few household utensils on the backs of horses, and each with as much as they could carry, they started from Londonderry the first of May.

Among the number was a young man, Phineas Spaulding, his wife, Phebe, who was a descendant of the famous Mrs. Dustin, and one child about one year and a half old.

They had not much to take with them, save stout hearts, and plenty of courage and hope.

The one precious thing Phebe had, was a copper tea-kettle, that had been brought from England by her mother, who was dead. This kettle, which would hold about three quarts, was packed full of packages of tea, pepper, spices and garden seeds, and was altogether too valuable to be entrusted out of her hands; so she started with her baby boy, Edward, in her arms, and carrying the tea-kettle, to walk a hundred and fifty miles.

She was a small, pretty looking woman, with brown hair and hazel eyes, and possessed wonderful power of endurance. She was graceful and agile in her movements. I have been told that when she wished to mount a horse, she would put her hand on his shoulder and jump from the ground to his back.

It was just at night-fall on the fifth day after this little party left Londonderry, that they approached the small settlement of Haverhill. The remainder of the way was through the wilderness, where their only guide would be marked trees. The emigrants were hospitably entertained by the people of Haverhill, and were urged to remain a few days and rest, but they were anxious to get to their journey's end, and only stayed one night.

In the hurry of getting started the next morning, Mrs. Spaulding put her baby on the floor, while she was arranging something, and he being left to himself, crept to the hearth and pulled a kettle of hot water over, and before his mother could reach him, his feet were scalded.

Of course this accident prevented Mrs. Spaulding from going on, and it was decided after a consultation with others, for her to remain a few days. It would be necessary for some one to return to Haverhill for some meal, so Mr. Spaulding told his wife to wait patiently, and he would come for her as soon as he could. Phebe saw her friends depart with much regret, and watched them until they were lost from sight in the wood.

It proved that the baby was not very badly burned, and Mrs. Spaulding was sorry that she had not gone on with the others, but she waited as patiently as she could, until the time had passed when her husband should have returned for her. As the days went by, and he did not come, she resolved she would wait no longer, but go on alone.

The people she was with, endeavored to persuade

her to remain until her husband came for her, but from all accounts, Phebe had a will of her own, and would not consent to remain, but started with her baby, and carrying the tea-kettle and a good supply of food, for a walk of fifty miles, through a dense woods. Undaunted by fear of wild animals or Indians, she marched bravely on, her only guide the spotted trees. Think of this young, but plucky little woman, starting with a helpless baby in her arms, and knowing she would have to remain over night in the woods, to walk through the wilderness alone.

On she went, noticing with pleasure, the signs of spring on every side. The brown buds just bursting, and the tender green leaves peeping out. She thought of the garden she would have, planted with the seeds she had in her tea-kettle. Then she would beguile the weary way, with snatches of songs or strains from some old hymns she had heard her mother sing, until I think the birds must have hushed their songs to listen to this strange music.

Just as the sun's declining rays gave warning that the day was almost gone, Phebe came to a pond, now called "Streeter's Pond," which she must ford; concluding to wait till morning before crossing, she began to look around for some place to spend the night. Presently the twisted trunk of an old hemlock caught her sight. It was crooked in such a way that it formed a kind of cradle. She fixed a bed out of some boughs and laid the baby, who was asleep, in this novel cradle. Then she dug a hole in the ground close by the tree, and put the tea-kettle in, covering it carefully, so the Indians, should they come, would not get it.

She ate her supper, and laid down by her baby, not meaning to go to sleep. Long she lay gazing up through the branches of the trees, at the stars twinkling in the sky, and listened to the hoot of the owl, and screech of the catamount, but her walk of twenty-five miles, and carrying the baby, had tired her so she could not keep awake, and commending her baby and herself to him " whose eye never slumbers or sleeps," she fell into a dreamless slumber.

When she awoke the day was breaking, and the birds had already commenced their morning concert. She arose from her uncomfortable bed, feeling lame and unrefreshed, but thankful the night had been passed in safety. She ate her breakfast, resurrected her tea-kettle, and was soon on her way. She was determined not to pass another night in the woods alone, and went on as far as she could, only stopping a little while to rest, and eat her dinner.

Just at dark, when she was beginning to think she would not be able to go on, as she could not see the marked trees, the path began to widen, and as she reached the top of a hill, she almost shouted for joy, for in a little valley at the foot of the hill, were a few log houses, and from the open door of one, she could see the cheerful gleams of firelight; how pleasant it looked to the chilled, exhausted woman. Pressing on, she directed her steps to that house, and was kindly received by the inmates; from them she learned that she had reached Lancaster, but her destination was six miles farther on. Gladly she accepted their hospitality until morning, when she finished her journey, arriving at Northumberland about noon, giving her husband, who was just making preparations to go for her, a great surprise. Phebe found her anxiety had been needless. Mr. Spaulding had delayed going back to Haverhill until he had put up a rude log house, so Phebe found a home awaiting her, and they were soon settled at housekeeping. Their furniture was of the rudest kind, all being home-made. But her tea-kettle sang just as cheerfully on her humble hearth, as it had done in her childhood's home, and she would sit before the fire, holding her baby, and think of the time when, instead of the woods that now encompassed their house, fields of waving grass and corn would be seen, and their log house exchanged for a nice framed building.

She had planted her garden, and already the seeds were springing up; but there were times when it looked very dark to the poor emigrants. The Indians were troublesome, food was not plenty, indeed their chief dependence was upon hunting and fishing. Some of the party were anxious to return to Londonderry, and Mr. Spaulding would have been easily persuaded to have done so, had it not been for his wife. It is said that she was setting out some cabbage plants in her garden one afternoon, when some of those who wished to return came to talk the matter over; but Phebe put her hoe down decidedly, and told them " all to go, every one; she never would."

She felt sure it only required patience and perseverance, to make that " wilderness blossom like the rose."

It happened one time during that first year, that Mr. Spaulding had gone hunting, to be gone two or three days, leaving Phebe and the baby alone. As it began to be dark, she thought she would take her baby and go to the nearest neighbor's, which was about a mile, but decided she would not be so foolish, and going to the door to close and fasten it, six Indians confronted her.

They had approached the house so noiselessly she had not heard them. Her heart sank within her as she saw them, but trying to speak as if she had no fear, she inquired what they wanted; they informed her; " they had come to her house to have a pow-wow." Probably surprise parties had not come in fashion then, and Phebe was rather embarrassed at the announcement, but knowing that she must not offend the Indians by refusing, bade them come in.

They seated themselves around the fire, inviting Phebe to join them, and not daring to refuse, she sat down with them, holding her baby in her arms. The Indians had plenty of " fire water," and commenced drinking, passing the bottle to Phebe, would say, " brave white squaw no 'fraid drink fire water." She would make a pretence of accepting their offer and to appear as if she was not frightened. For hours the Indians kept up a perfect bedlam, until one by one they were overcome by the " fire water," and sank into a drunken stupor. Through the whole night Mrs. Spaulding sat there holding her child.

In the morning the Indians aroused from their sleep and crept out of the house. Ever after that

Mrs. Spaulding was considered a heroine by them, and called the "brave white squaw," and they expressed their admiration of her behavior to them, by bringing her presents of game, fish and corn. Mrs. Spaulding's dream was fulfilled; she saw the wilderness disappear before the ax of the woodman, and thrifty farms and comfortable homes take its place.

She lived to be about eighty, leaving many descendants to cherish her memory. The copper teakettle is in the possession of a great-great-granddaughter, who considers it one of her household treasures.

THE DRIVE AROUND MT. PROSPECT

Of all short drives in this vicinity, the one around Mt. Prospect affords the grandest mountain views.

We drive up the Sand Hill, and along the Jefferson road for a mile, passing on the right, Holton Hill, and on the left, getting a charming view of the Pilot range, and the "out east" part of the town. We also notice, close to the roadside on the left, a number of acres of smooth green grass, sloping toward Israel's river, whose course through the narrow valley can be traced by the trees and bushes that fringe its banks; this land is quite a contrast to the rugged rocky pastures on either side of it, which are samples of what this was, before the rocks and stones had been removed, and built into the substantial wall that surrounds it. Just in front, we get a grand view of the White Mountains.

Presently we arrive at a road leading to the right, which is our way. We now have Mt. Pleasant directly in front, Mt. Prospect a little to the left of it. The road is gradually ascending until we arrive at the " Freeman place," on the top of the hill. From this point we get a most beautiful view of the cultivated land, extending from the base half way up the side of Mt. Prospect. A maple grove, enclosed by a stone wall, stands stately and graceful, among the patches of corn, yellow rye and half ripened oats, and above all the tree-crowned summit of the mountain, making a most perfect landscape picture. A short distance beyond the " Freeman place," we turn to the left, and are on the direct road around Mt. Prospect.

How delightfully shady and pleasant it is! What a profusion of growth there is about us! Moisture and the right proportion of light and shade, give here the best conditions for the growth of the fern, which can be found in the woods on the right, grow ing in great quantities and variety. The rare specimen known as the maiden hair, is found here in abundance; this locality is quite noted as the only place in the vicinity of Lancaster where this fern can be found.

As we go on, the trees on either side increase in size, until the over hanging branches almost meet. The birds seem to think the top of these swaying trees a splendid place to practice their songs; the "dim woods" ring with their blithesome singing, and the red squirrel runs about in a pert, nimble way, or sits up to nibble a choice bit he has found, with his tail held gracefully over his back. On the right, we notice among the trees, masses or ledges of rocks, piled in some places to a considerable height, covered with beautiful green moss; in some places the rents and fissures contain soil, from which shrubs and even small trees are growing. Emerging from this lovely piece of woods, we come to a breadth of open country. On the left, beyond the undulating acres of the farm now owned by Mr. Johnson, but originally settled and occupied for many years by a man known as "Quaker Eastman," we can see the village of Jefferson, with Mt. Starr King, rising above it; a little to the right is Bray Hill, and towering grandly over all, are the White and Franconia mountain ranges.

We drive on, passing on the right a brook, that comes hurrying down the hillside, as if in haste to join the "brimming river." Now we pass on the left, the "old Lovejoy farm," long the home of Abial Lovejoy, father of John Lovejoy, a former resident of Lancaster. The place is now owned by Mr. Alexander.

On the opposite side a little farther along, we arrive at the Bucknam place. This farm was settled by Edward Bucknam, and was his home during his life. Mrs. Sarah Bucknam, his widow, is still living in the old home, at the advanced age of ninety-seven, and is, I am informed, the oldest woman in town. She retains her memory in a remarkable manner, and can read, sew and knit, as well as many much younger women. This farm is now in the possession of Mr. Jacobs, a son-in-law of Mrs. Bucknam. The quantity and quality of the butter made on this farm, is quite celebrated.

On the same side of the road a few rods beyond, we come to the old Week's place, which is situated on the slope, but near the base of Mt. Prospect, and is now known as "Prospect farm." This place was settled and house erected by James B. Weeks, father of Judges James W. and William D. Weeks. In what used to be the kitchen, the original fireplace still remains; and in the front hall, there is a stair-case and railing, made by Judge James W. Weeks.

In selecting this situation, on which to build his house, Mr. Weeks certainly displayed a taste for grand mountain scenery. There is not a spot in town, where the White Mountain and Franconia ranges can be seen so boldly outlined, as from this raised plateau in front of Prospect farm house. A broad sweep of rolling hills, pastures and cultivated fields, with stately groves of maple and dark pine, stretch away for miles in front of the house. Beyond, on the left, we see Jefferson village with the Pilot range for a back-ground, nearly in front Bray Hill and Cherry Mountain, on the left the village of Bethlehem with Mt. Agassiz just beyond it. Majestically rising above all, are the White and Franconia mountains, at just the right distance to display the confederate strength of the chain, and mellow the gorges and ravines that channel their sides into beauty and grandeur. We need no telescope to enable us to see the road winding up Mt. Washington, and the house at the top is plainly discernable. The long serrated summit of Mt. Lafayette is seen to better advantage from this point, than from any place we know of in this vicinity. Many years ago, there used to be a beaver meadow on the opposite side of the road from this house, but all traces of it have long since disappeared.

Many improvements have been made at Prospect Farm the last few years by the present owner, Mr. George P. Rowell. Stones and rocks removed from the land and built into substantial walls. Trees planted. A flower garden artistically laid out. A beautiful maple grove just back of the house cleared of underbrush, and with hammocks and seats, affords a charming retreat for a summer day. Commodious barns and out-buildings have been erected, and short-horned cattle, Shropshire-down sheep, and Berkshire swine, are taking the place of the common stock.

Reluctantly we turn away from this grand view, and drive on. We are now on the opposite side of Mt. Prospect, the road winding along between Mt. Prospect and Pleasant. The view driving down this road to the village, it is *down* all the way, is very lovely, and quite different from the prospect we had going. We now see broad meadows extending for miles toward the north and west, the Connecticut winding in graceful curves through the green verdure; beyond the tree-crowned hills, rise the mountain ranges of Vermont, the hazy summits mingling with the wonderful blue of the summer sky.

The houses of the village clustering in the valley, the red roof of the Lancaster House easily distinguished from the others. The tapering church spires pointing upward, and all illuminated with a golden glow, from the sun, slowly sinking behind the hills, make another beautiful picture to hang on the walls of our memory.

We come into the village from the Whitefield road, and drive down the Sand Hill, rattle over the bridge, reaching our home as

> " All the sky is grand with clouds,
> And athwart the evening air
> Wheel the swallows home in crowds."

OUR " BUNKER HILL.

Probably there are many in our village, who are not familiar with the story which caused the hill on the left of Summer street to receive the appelation of " Bunker Hill."

The facts in regard to the origin of the name are as follows:

Many years ago there resided in our town a man of great muscular strength, who from his youth up had been the conqueror in feats of strength and wrestling matches.

The Fourth of July and muster days, were occasions on which he displayed his prowess, and won his laurels.

One fall, when the annual muster was in progress on Holton meadow, and people had come in large numbers to witness the military display, this man, whom I have mentioned, met his first rival.

There appeared that day upon the scene, a man of splendid physique, young and agile. He had recently returned from a whaling voyage, and altogether was considered quite a hero. Very jealously this young athlete was watched as he displayed his gymnastic powers, by the man who was no longer young, but who until to-day had born the palm of victory alone; now he must admit he had a rival.

It was suggested, that there should be a wrestling match between these two, but the older man decided that was not the place for a real trial of strength. Before the day had passed, it had been arranged in a confidential manner between these two, that they would meet the next morning at sunrise, on the hill

I have mentioned, and settle which was the best man in a good square fight.

It chanced that a boy overheard the making of this arrangement, and before sunrise next morning, many a stump, stone and tree, on the hill, concealed an expectant spectator. Punctually the men arrived on the spot, and a hard contested battle was fought, resulting in the defeat of the veteran of so many fights and wrestling matches.

This was too much for the boys, who burst into a loud hurrah, as they scampered down the hill to tell the great news that Old Blank had been whipped at last.

Ever since that morning the scene of this contest has been called " Bunker Hill."

THE DRIVE TO EGYPT.

Of the two beautiful meadow drives in this vicinity, perhaps the one to " Egypt " through the Connecticut river meadows, to the " William Weeks place," affords more variety of scenery than the one to the " Stockwell meadows:" however, both are most charming drives. In going to " Egypt," we leave the village by the Baker Hill, taking the second turn to the right, we soon pass, on the left, the old arsenal; being no longer required for the storehouse of war-like equipments, it has become the peaceful abode of Mr. Streeter's horse.

Directly in front is a beautiful view of rolling meadows, and further on the green hills of Vermont. On the right the " twin peaks " stand like sentinels guarding Cape Horn.

We soon arrive at a point where the road diverges to the right and left. The left is our way. Just at the turn we pass on the right, on a sunny hillside, the Catholic cemetery. We are now on the road to " Egypt." This title arising, so I am informed, by the failure, many years ago, of the corn crop in this town, save that which was planted in this vicinity, which grew in a remarkable way and yielded abundantly.

As the people were obliged to come here for corn, they were probably reminded of the story in the Old Testament of Joseph's brethren who were sent to Egypt to buy corn. In this way the name was acquired, and ever since, the drive in this direction has been called "going to Egypt." The road is level and smooth, bordered on each side by green fields, radiant with buttercups and elder flowers.

We soon come to the " Chessman place " on the right. This farm was first settled by a man by the name of Bruce. Just on the opposite side of the road is the " Brooks farm."

The highway ends here, but by the courtesy of the owners of the land, people are allowed to drive on by the bank of the river and through the meadow, to the highway.

On our right the shining river rolls along, its banks o'erhung with alders and birch. Just on the other side we see the old Hopkins place, now owned by the Rhodes brothers.

Eighteen noble elms stand gracefully grouped together in the foreground, making a beautiful and conspicuous feature in the landscape. Long may they be spared from the relentless ax and saw.

On our left the broad meadow rolls away for a mile. Dancing shadows of light and shade from the great banks of soft, white clouds, that float majestically through the sky, chase each other over the billowy grass.

Gradually the ground rises from this green plane, and we see the farms on the slope of Mt. Pleasant and Stebbins' hill. The color of the different harvests contrast pleasantly with the dark green of the pine trees that cover the hillsides. Above all, Mt. Prospect looks down like some patriarch over the wide family of hills settled comfortably about him.

Far away to the west the horizon is framed with hills, the most distant seem to touch " high heaven," and lose themselves amid the clouds.

We drive on through this sea of green, arriving at the South Lancaster road just by the " Weeks place."

Turning to our left, we are on the way to the village, soon passing on our right the " Brackett place," and on the left the farms of Messrs. Hilliard and Woodward, formerly owned by Rowell brothers.

Going along another mile and a half, we see the village cosily situated along a level plane, just under the rim of the hills, presenting from this view an entirely different aspect than from Sand Hill.

From the top of Baker Hill we get a fine point of the White Mountains and Pilot range.

This drive should be considered one of the most delightful short drives, affording as it does, varied and charming views of river, meadows and mountains.

A TRUE STORY.

The following incident which I am about to re-late is true, but all who were interested in the oc-currence, save one, departed many years ago, on that "long journey from whence none ever return."

No doubt all who are acquainted with the sur-roundings of the village, have noticed four very handsome elm trees, that stand near a little brook, on the south-east corner of the lot now owned by Parker J. Noyes. These trees were set out about seventy years ago, by a woman of the name of Hart, who had a rude little cottage near there.

No trace of the humble home remains. The hands that brought the little saplings from the woods, and planted them by her door, have long since mouldered into dust, but the trees are stand-ing, graceful and stately monuments to her memory, and the brook still chatters over the stones, singing as it goes,

"Men may come, and men may go,
But I go on forever."

In the year 1812, there was living in Canada a man and wife by name of Hart. Their home had formerly been in Massachusetts, but for some rea-son they had removed to Canada. Mr. Hart had purchased a good farm, and these people, who were no longer young, had every prospect of spending their declining days in comfort and prosperity, but all these anticipations were destroyed, by the declaration of the war of 1812, which occurred on the 18th of June of that year.

Soon an edict from the king, proclaiming that the property of all the citizens of Canada, who would not take arms against the United States, should be confiscated to the crown. Although it must have been a hard decision, Mr. Hart did not hesitate to relinquish all the property he had, rather than espouse the cause of the enemies of his native land.

Leaving his home, he started with his wife for the States. Having relatives residing at Jefferson, N. H., he decided to go there; but the loss of his property, together with bad health, so preyed upon his mind, that within a short time he became insane. Mr. Hart lived a few years in this unfortunate condition. His wife took care of him, and did what she could toward their support, his relations assisting her. After his death, she decided to go to Lancaster to live, hoping to get more work to do there.

The rude cottage, consisting of only one room,

was built for her, on the spot I have mentioned, and she took possession of it, living there a number of years, supporting herself by spinning and weaving, receiving gratefully the presents of food and other things, that kind people sent her.

Mrs. Hart was a woman of some education, and as I am informed, "a good Christian," believing firmly in the teachings of the Bible; but in the course of time she grew rather eccentric, living so much alone, and like many elderly people, dreamed dreams and saw visions. With the passing years she grew very infirm, but still she lived on in her little home, though she seemed to be too aged to be left alone.

Some may inquire why a poor and almost helpless woman, was left to live in this way. In those days, there were no comfortable places for such people to go to. The poor were put up at public auction, to be bid off by the lowest bidder, who was to board them, at the expense of the town.

Mrs. Hart, who had once been in good circumstances, still had considerable pride, and would not consent to be sold at auction, like a bale of goods, or live stock.

One cold morning, late in the fall, a boy about twelve years of age, started with his gun on his shoulder, for a walk through the woods, hoping to find some partridges or other game.

As he came in the vicinity of Mrs. Hart's house, he could hear boys laughing and shouting, " Why don't you get up, you old witch ? " Hastening on, he soon came in sight of two boys, about his own age, who were throwing stones into the brook, and splashing the cold water upon Mrs. Hart, who had fallen, in attempting to dip a pail of water from the brook. The ground being frozen and icy along the bank, she had fallen in such a way that her feet were submerged in the water.

Calling out to the boys to desist in their cruel conduct, John, as we will call him, ran to the assistance of the poor old woman.

With great difficulty he got her up, and partly carrying and partly dragging her, got her into her house, and on the bed.

Mrs. Hart was so exhausted, with cold and fright, that she could hardly speak. John saw that the fire in the little fireplace was out, and there was no wood to rekindle it. He went out and collected some sticks, made a good fire, and then asked Mrs. Hart if she had anything to eat in the house. She replied, " Not much—some potatoes." Boys, sixty years ago, did not have much money, but John had a silver " fo-pence half penny " piece in his pocket, one he had kept for a long time. Telling Mrs. Hart he would soon return, he ran down the hill to the first store he came to, and exchanged his silver piece for some crackers. These he carried back to the old woman, whom he found sitting by the fire, trying to dry her wet clothing. Having now done all he could for her comfort, he was about to leave, when Mrs. Hart raised her withered hand and bade him come to her. "John," she said, " remember the words of an old woman, whose sands of life are almost run. I should have died by the brook-side, with the laughter and jeering remarks of those wicked boys ringing in my ears, had it not been for you, but it has been my death blow. I want you to listen to what I am about to say, and remember it is the prophecy of a dying woman:"

"I see you, as in a vision, growing up to manhood, respected by all. You will become prosperous; land and money will be yours; a happy home, with wife and children to be a blessing and comfort to you, and your days will be long upon the earth; but those boys who saw me, stooping with age and infirmity, slip on the icy ground, and instead of coming to my assistance, threw stones, and derided me with laughter and scorn, the judgment of God will follow. A comfortable or happy home, neither will ever have, and disgrace and ruin will follow their footsteps. You will live to see this fulfilled, and remembering what has happened to-day, acknowledge my prophecy proved correct." Mrs. Hart uttered these words in a very impressive manner.

Soon after, John left the cottage, and thought as he walked away, that he would always remember what the old woman had said.

He was a poor boy, and had not any faith that such a good fortune could be for him. The next day a neighbor, who went to see Mrs. Hart, found the door fastened, and receiving no answer to repeated raps, burst the door open, and found the old lady lying upon her bed, insensible. Other neighbors were called in, and the doctor sent for, but all efforts to arouse her proved unavailing. It was decided to move her to a more comfortable place. She was carried to a house near by, where, within two days, she died.

More than fifty years have passed since the death of Mrs. Hart. What has become of the three boys, whose future she predicted? Singular as it may seem, the prophecy has been fulfilled.

One, soon after reaching manhood, committed a

criminal offense, and was sentenced to a long term
in the state prison, where he died before the expir-
ation of the sentence.

The other grew up, worthless and dissipated,
and his last days were spent in the poor house.

John, by hard work, economy and temperance,
acquired a competence. Is now surrounded by all
the comforts of life. A good wife and children
make his declining days happy, and he is an hon-
ored citizen of our town.

THE SOLILOQUY OF THE OLD ACADEMY.

Surely this is a world of change; when I look
back over my past life, and recall all I have been
through, I wonder there is an original board left on
my frame.

It seldom falls to the lot of a building, to experience the vicissitudes that I have. When I was new!
Ah, me! how long ago! I stood at the north end
of the village, and was known as the court house.
To be sure I was not a very handsome building, but
many far more elegant edifices have not sheltered
people of the talent and education I have.

I can recall with pride, the names of Daniel Webster, Levi Woodbury, Ichabod Bartlett, Joseph Bell and others, whose voices have been heard within my walls.

I was not only used for a court house, but also for religious services by the Methodist society, before their church was built, and have been occupied by the Masonic Fraternity. It will not do for me to reveal the remarkable scenes I have witnessed during their meetings, or I might in my old age share the fate of John Morgan.

After a number of years, it was considered necessary to build a new court house; about that time the people were talking of starting a high school, and it was thought best to convert me into an academy. This was done, and for several years I was used for that purpose on the spot above mentioned. After a while it was decided to remove me to a more central location; accordingly I was taken down the street, to the spot where the academy now stands. I did not so very much mind the journey. I was, comparatively speaking, young then, and rather liked the idea of a change.

I stood the trip very well, although I must admit I got a pretty severe shaking, and was very glad to get settled.

I was somewhat enlarged, new desks were put in.

A steeple was built, in which a bell was hung, which is now on the graded school building.

I remember with pride, the large number of learned and accomplished gentlemen, who taught the school during the years I was the " academy." Every day, men and women pass me, who received most of their education beneath my roof, and many have gone forth into the " great world," but I have no doubt memory often reverts to the peaceful shades of this village, and happy school days, passed in the " old academy."

With the passing years, I became old-fashioned, and rather dilapidated, and it was considered best to have a new building for the school; so I was sold to a society known as " Baptists," and was moved farther down the street, and on the opposite side. I felt sorry to leave the spot where I had stood so long, and where I had hoped to spend my days. I was then completely remodeled. The old desks were removed, new windows put in, and pews made, an alcove and raised platform were built at one end, on which a pulpit was placed. At the right of the pulpit was an orchestra, where an organ was put, a carpet was laid down, and church furniture put in. I felt rather proud of my appearance, when all was accomplished, I was no longer the " old academy," but the " Baptist church."

My prosperity, however, was short-lived. Meetings were held quite regularly for a while, but I conclude from what I overheard, that the financial condition of the society was rather low. They could not support a minister. Occasionally a service would be held, but they became less and less frequent and farther apart, until they finally ceased.

Then came a sad period in my life. One who has been useful, dislikes to find themselves stand for nothing in a community. I was occasionally used for temperance or prayer meetings, but most of the time I was left lonely and sad, with plenty of time to repent of my vanity, and the airs I had assumed, at being converted into a church.

After a few years I passed out of the hands of the Baptist society, but still remained useless.

One day I was aroused from the stupid condition into which I had fallen, by having my doors and window blinds thrown open. Some men came and commenced to take out the pews. I wondered what was going to happen, and listened attentively to their talk. I soon discovered another change awaited me. I was to be made into an " armory." What a life they do lead me! I thought; but still I had rather wear out than rust out.

All appearance of a church disappeared. A nice

hard wood floor was laid down, and soon I began
to present a very war-like appearance. Soldiers'
accoutrements were placed about my walls, and my
floor resounded to the martial tread of armed men.
I was now an " armory," and should have been
rather proud, only I remembered my experience as
" church." An entire change now took place in
my life.

Instead of religious services, dances and merry-
makings were in order. I will admit I was shocked
at first, at the idea of turning a church into a dancing hall, but soon found out I was old-fashioned in
my notions, and resigned myself to my fate.

During the time I was an " armory," I was frequently used for other things. Ice cream festivals,
sewing circles, sociables, etc., but the most surpris-
ing thing of all, was the roller skating. The jars
and severe treatment I received by those people,
was something awful, and the noise nearly made
me crazy. I was only too thankful when it was
decided to go where there was more room.

I should have had a very dull time after that, only for some musical rehearsals, which I enjoyed
very much.

One day as I was thinking over the past, and re-
gretting that I could not be made more useful in my

old age, I heard some men come in. They commenced to take down the guns and other soldierly equipments, and carry them out.

" What's coming now? " I thought. Again I listened to the conversation, and was astonished to hear I was going to be a " public library! "

Workmen soon began to put up book-shelves, and make other alterations, to fit me for the new position I was to occupy.

I think the painting of my exterior has given me more pleasure than anything that has been done. I was getting so shabby I was really ashamed of myself. The color is so suitable for my age, too, " neat but not gaudy."

I declare, it makes me feel quite chipper, to think I am to have such an honorable position. I trust that after all my trying experiences, my last days may be passed as a library, but after what I have been through, I am prepared for anything.

THE OLD ACADEMY.

THE DRIVE AROUND THE GORE

Who that has taken the drive around the Gore does not remember it with pleasure? We leave the village by Middle street. The road is gradually ascending until we reach the " Bush farm." From this point, the view is exceedingly lovely. On the left is the Pilot range, towering over the intervening hills. These mountains seem to be a favorite ground for shadows, and from here the mantle of spotted light and shade that envelop them, is admirably displayed. In front, the road can be seen winding along for some distance, bordered on either side with pleasant, homelike looking houses. On the right are the undulating meadows of Israel's river, whose circuitous course can be easily traced through the green verdure, by the trees and bushes that overhang its banks. This little valley is one of the pleasantest places in Lancaster—shut in on either side by hills, piled together in every way that is picturesque.

We soon pass on our left, the " Freeman place," originally the home of Samuel White, father of Nathaniel White, who left his home at an early age, for Concord, N. H. Arriving there with only one shilling in his pocket, by industry, economy and temperance, he accumulated a large fortune.

We drive along the smooth, hard road, passing, on the left by the " Weeks place," a long row of tamarack trees, which were set out many years ago by Mr. Hemminway, a former owner of the place. On our right is the little brick house, known for many years as the " Whipple place." The brick-yard, which used to be on the opposite side of the road, has disappeared.

On we go, passing the pleasant homes of the Spauldings, crossing the bridge over the "great brook," we ascend the hill by the " Smith place." On the right is a charming view of Mt. Prospect and Pleasant, and the farm-houses and orchards, on the south road leading to Jefferson.

Passing the Stalbird and Savage places, we arrive at the " Cummings farm," where the road curves to the left. On the right is a grand and extensive view. Beyond the swells and rolls of land, Jefferson Mills is seen, somewhat to the left are the houses of Jefferson Hill, and rising above all, the glistening summits of the White Mountains.

The north road can be seen the whole distance, and the cleared land, patches of grain and corn on the slope and base of the Pilot range, all making a beautiful landscape picture of

" Cultivated slopes, and tracts of forest ground and scattered
  groves,
And mountains bare, or clothed with ancient forests."

Before reaching the " Stillings place," the road is

bordered on either side for some distance with beautiful maple trees. Whoever planted them, deserves to be gratefully remembered. Leaving the road to Jefferson, we are on the direct way around the Gore.

Very soon we enter one of the most beautiful pieces of woods in Lancaster. The road, white and hard, stretches away like the aisle of a cathedral, and is lost beneath the leafy arches of maple and beech.

Emerging from this lovely place, and crossing a little bridge that spans another portion of the great brook, Garland's mills are seen on the left, and we presently pass a neat cottage house, recently erected by E. C. Garland, who is experimenting in hatching chickens by artificial incubation.

Driving on, we presently pass a beautiful maple grove on the hillside at the left, known as "Pilot Heights Grove," a favorite place for picnics.

On the right, beyond the cultivated land, are acres of primeval forest, as yet untouched by the ax of the woodman. Above and beyond these woods, Percy Peaks and Cape Horn are boldly outlined against the sky.

Passing the Plaisted and Stockwell farms, we hear the hum of a saw-mill, and very soon we see on the right Stockwell's mills and the Grange. Another mile brings us into the "out east" road just by the "Week's place." From here we return on the same road by which we left the village, and finish our delightful drive, just as

> "Slowly o'er the pleasant landscape
> Falls the evening's dusk and coolness."

THE FARRAR HOUSE MYSTERY.

The house in which the following remarkable event occurred, was situated on the spot where the Catholic parsonage now stands, and was known as the Farrar house.

It is only a few years since this house, which was a large two-story building, was taken down, and there are many, now living in town, who knew the Farrar family, but as far as I have been able to ascertain, the only one now living in the village, who was here in 1818, the year in which this incident transpired, is Mrs. Allen Smith, who was a girl of eighteen at that time, and was teaching school here. She was familiar with the whole affair, and I am indebted to her for the following account.

At the time I am writing of, this house was occu-

pied by Deacon Farrar and wife, a young man by
name of George Kibby, a relative of Mrs. Farrar's,
and a young girl, Hannah Nute, who assisted Mrs.
Farrar about the housework. She was a small,
delicate looking girl, with very pretty blue eyes,
and brown hair.

Deacon Farrar, as his name indicates, was deacon
of the Congregational church, a lawyer by profession, and had for some years been clerk of the court.
He was a small, spare man, very agreeable and
pleasant in his manners. Besides discharging his
duties as deacon, he was also a member of the choir,
and played upon a very large bass viol.

Mrs. Farrar was a tall, thin woman, with dark
hair, which she wore arranged in little curls at each
side of her face; and she always wore a turban-
shaped cap, which gave her a very majestic appearance. She was very dignified in her manners, and
a little inclined to be aristocratic; but a most excel-
lent woman, and a devout member of the church.

Hannah Nute occupied a bedroom on the ground
floor and opening out of the kitchen, the other mem-
bers of the family slept up-stairs. One night Hannah was awakened by hearing a loud rap under
her bed. She was much startled, but thinking it
might be the rats in the cellar, was just going to

sleep, when she was again disturbed by hearing three distinct raps in the same place. Thoroughly aroused and frightened, she jumped from her bed, ran through the kitchen to the hall, and up the stairs, calling, " Oh! Mrs. Farrar, Mrs. Farrar," as she fell almost fainting at her chamber door.

" What do you mean, Hannah, by giving me such a fright? I thought the house was on fire," said Mrs. Farrar, opening the door.

" There is some one under my bed," said Hannah, gasping for breath.

" What nonsense, you have been dreaming."

" Oh, no! I wan't asleep, and they rapped three times very loud on the floor."

" Oh, Hannah, I am surprised that you should be so foolish, but come, I will go down with you and look under your bed."

" Oh, hadn't you better get the deacon to go and look, I am sure some one is there?" but Mrs. Farrar was already half way down stairs, and with fear and trembling, Hannah followed her. Mrs. Farrar stopped in the kitchen and lighted a candle by the coals that were still brightly glowing on the hearth, and going into Hannah's room looked under the bed. Hannah had not ventured into the room.

" Come here and look for yourself. Now are

you convinced you were dreaming?" said Mrs. Farrar, as Hannah stepped into the room. Just at that moment, three distinct raps came, apparently from beneath the girl's feet.

She gave a loud scream and ran into the kitchen, Mrs. Farrar following rather quickly for her.

" Oh, some one is in the cellar, do call the deacon," said Hannah.

Just then George Kibby, who had been awakened by Hannah's screams, came rushing into the kitchen, calling out, "What is the matter?" closely followed by the deacon, who said, " Why, wife! what is this commotion? "

Mrs. Farrar explained the cause of this unusual excitement, and as if to corroborate her statement, there came a succession of loud raps on the kitchen floor.

" There," screamed Hannah.

" This is really alarming," said Mrs. Farrar.

" I will soon find out what is making this disturbance," said the deacon, taking the long iron fire-shovel in one hand, and the candlestick in the other, and starting for the cellar door. George took the tongs and followed, Mrs. Farrar brandishing a broom, and Hannah, with a big stick of wood, brought up the rear. The cellar was thoroughly searched, but nothing was discovered.

By this time they were all very much alarmed. A fire was built in the kitchen, and they gathered around it to talk the matter over.

"Deacon," said Mrs. Farrar, " I think it is a warning. I have heard of such things."

" I think that the house is haunted," said George.

" Well," said the deacon, " it is certainly a singular and startling phenomenon, and I think George had better go for Parson Willard."

" Perhaps it is best," said Mrs. Farrar.

Meanwhile the rapping continued at short intervals. Hannah became almost prostrated with fright, the neighbors were sent for, and in the early morning the parson came; he could offer no explanation for the remarkable disturbance.

It was thought proper under the circumstances to hold a religious service, the great family Bible was brought from the parlor, and a portion of the Scriptures read, and prayers offered, but still the raps were heard.

A thorough investigation of the house and cellar was made, and the blinds on the outside examined; but nothing could be found to throw the least light on this mysterious rapping. It was, however, as-

certained that the raps only came in the room where
Hannah was, and seemed to follow her; some persons thought she must in some way cause them. As
the days went by and there was no cessation of
this rapping, the whole town became excited; the
house was thronged with people from this, and the
adjoining towns, who came to visit the " haunted
house."

As many of the people in the village were of the
opinion that Hannah Nute must in some way cause
the raps, it was decided to have her watched, and
four of the leading men of the town were appointed as an investigating committee. They tied the
girl's hands and feet, and laid her on a bed, they
then sat down by her, two on each side of the bed.
In that way she was watched for a day and night,
but meanwhile the raps were heard, on the walls
and floor, and even on the bedstead, but only in the
room where Hannah was.

The committee decided that they could not in any
way account for the raps. Some of the people
thought it was a warning to the family of some
misfortune that would shortly follow, while others
said it must be the work of the devil. The knowl-
edge of knowing that she was suspected of making
the raps, had made Hannah quite ill, and she beg-

ged to be sent away. On the day she left the house, the raps were more frequent than they had been, and as she passed through the hall to the door, seemed to follow her, and came with great force on the floor, but that was the last of the raps, whatever it was that caused them, whether

"Good spirits or bad,
Black spirits or white,"

seemed to leave the house when Hannah did.

Deacon Farrar and family occupied the house for many years after, and never were troubled by a repetition of this remarkable occurrence, which has always remained unexplained, and the rappings at the Farrar house are still spoken of as a great mystery.

THE DRIVE TO THE TOP OF MT. PROSPECT.

The drive to the top of Mount Prospect is very pleasant, and easily and safely accomplished by the good carriage-road, that has been made quite to the top by W. H. Smith, who has built a comfortable hotel, large enough to accommodate thirty-five guests, on the summit of this mountain.

Leaving the village by the Sand Hill, we drive along the Whitefield road for a mile and a half, when we take a road leading to the left. Another half mile brings us to the little toll-house at the foot of the mountain, from here to the top of the mountain the distance is three-quarters of a mile. The first of the way is only slightly ascending; as we go on, we come to some steep pitches, but our horses have no difficulty in taking us safely over them. The road winds in such a way that the house is not visible until we turn the last curve, when we come right upon it. The genial landlord, Mr. W. H. Smith, stands on the steps to receive us, and we are soon landed on the broad piazza.

Mount Prospect is 2090 feet above tide-water, 1240 feet above Lancaster village. From the front piazza of the hotel we see in the foreground Cherry Mountain and, beyond, the whole Presidential range, crowned in the center by the dome of Mt. Washington. The belts of pine, and farther up, the gorges and ravines that sear the mountain's sides, are easily discerned. The railway and Summit House on Mt. Washington can be readily distinguished without the aid of a telescope. On the right we look down on Mt. Pleasant, Mt. Orne and Martin meadow pond, glistening like a great mirror in a setting of green hills that hem it in on all sides. Just between these mountains, but far in the distance, can be seen the tapering spire of a church in Lunenburg. Turning toward the north-west, we see the broad valley of the Connecticut, whose course can be traced for forty miles in sweeping curves through the luxuriant intervals and by hills clothed with forests, as with stately grace it flows down to the sea. Just in the foreground are the farms of Howe, Hodgdons, and the Daniel Stebbins' place, now known as the " Smith farm." The patches of corn, grain, groves of maple and pine, the farm-houses shaded by apple-trees, and farther on beyond the rolling hills, the village of Lancaster, cosily situated in the valley below, all make a beautiful picture. One might almost imagine, as they gaze down upon this scene of peace, plenty and purity, that it was some nook of primitive Eden, but " distance lends enchantment to the view."

Six villages, four hundred farms, and thirteen ponds, can be seen from the top of Mount Prospect, all surrounded by a mighty chain of mountains seven hundred miles in length. It is quite impossible for us to describe the extensive panorama of charming views that are presented from this mountian. The outlook is grand in every direction. In order to fully enjoy the trip, one should remain over night and witness the gorgeous beauties of the sunset and sunrise.

We see no reason why "Hotel Prospect" should not become a favorite resort. The cool bracing air will bring healing to the invalid, and the marvelous beauty of the view afford peace and rest to the weary.

The drive down the mountain and to the village is quickly accomplished, as it is nearly all the way descending. The sun is just sinking behind the Vermont hills, shedding a golden splendor over the meadows, and tinging the Pilot range and Percy Peaks with rose-color, as we drive down Sand Hill into the village.

GREAT GRANDMA'S CARPET.

The following sketch, although written in the form of a story, is strictly true. The grand-mother was Mrs. Persis Everett, wife of Judge Everett, and the carpet was made for a room in what is now known as the "Cross house." The writer has seen pieces of the carpet.

"Mother," said Annie Belmont, "It is a lovely

morning.   Don't you want to go down to Porter &
Gray's and choose our new carpets?   You know
we must get them down before cousin Dora comes
next week."

" Yes, I will go with you; but I must write some
letters first.   I will be ready in an hour."

" Annie," said Grandma Belmont, who was sitting by the fire knitting, " while your mother is
writing, don't you want me to tell you how my
mother got a carpet? "

" Oh, yes, grandma!   You know there is nothing I like so well as having you tell an old-fashioned
story."

" Well, my dear, you know, seventy-five years
ago, carpets were not very common.   Very few
people had them.   There was none made in this
country, and an English carpet was very expensive."

" What did you have on the floors, grandma? "

" Nothing—not even paint; but they were scoured
white as sand could make them.   My mother had
only one carpet in the house, and that was on the
parlor floor.   It was a green and black English carpet.   I suppose my mother made the first carpet
that was ever manufactured in New Hampshire, or
even in New England.   Your great-grandfather
was a lawyer, and, at that time, Lancaster was not

a shire town; the courts were held at Haverhill.
But after a while, Lancaster was made a shire town.
When father came home from the spring term of
court at Haverhill, he said the next fall the court
would sit in Lancaster, and as there was no suitable
place for the judges to board, he had promised to
take them in. They used to have three judges—
the chief justice and two side judges. I am sure I
don't know what they were called side judges for,
unless it was because one sat on each side of the
judge who attended to all the business. I have often been into court with father, and I never heard
one say a word. They just sat there and looked
wise. Mother was surprised enough when father
said he was going to board the judges.

'Why, father,' she said, 'what are you thinking
of? There is not room enough in the house.'

'No,' said father, 'but there will be by fall. I
am going to have an addition of two rooms built on
to the house.'

'I don't see,' said mother, 'how we can get carpets; but if you are going to have the judges board
here, I will see what can be done.'

It was not very long before father had some men
at work on the new rooms, and mother began to
think something must be done about the carpets.

So she went up to see Eunice Stockwell, and talked it over with her. She was the best hand to weave there was anywhere round.

We had lots of sheep and plenty of wool, so mother took forty pounds and had it carded into rolls. Then she got Nancy Greenleaf and Lucy White to come and spin it.

It was spun into good strong yarn, four skeins to a pound. I was a little girl, but it seems to me I can see Nancy and Lucy now, just as they looked spinning. They had their wheels up in the great open chamber. It was in summer time, and the windows were open at each end of the room. I used to go up there and sit on an old chest by the window, and watch them spin. Nancy was tall and slim, and had light hair, which she wore done up in a little ball on the top of her head, fastened with a big comb. She wore her dresses quite short, and as she stepped back and forth turning her wheel, she was always singing. I never heard her vary the tune or words:

" Come, Philander, let's be marching.'

She would come down heavy on the ' ching.' Who Philander was, or where he was going to march, I never could find out. I used to ask her to sing some more, but she said that was all she knew.

Lucy was a real pretty girl; she had black eyes and red cheeks; she used to make fun of Nancy and her song. Well, in a few weeks, the spinning was all done; then mother had the yarn carried up to Eunice Stockwell to be woven, and before long it was sent home—a great roll of white flannel. Then it had to be carried to Haverhill, to be fulled and colored. It was about thirty miles to Haverhill, and the only way to go was on horseback. Job, who was one of the hired men, packed it on to a horse, and started with it.

Meantime, mother had been coloring yarn—red, yellow, green and blue. She had to make all her dyes herself, but she had some bright, handsome colors. I remember how pretty it looked, hanging out on the line drying.

After a while, the cloth came home—three great rolls of dark brown, heavy cloth. Then it was cut into breadths, the length of the room, and mother and Aunt Betsy marked them off into squares, about a foot each way, so they would match when it was sewed together.

In each square was a large star. It was worked in what you call Kensington stitch. That's nothing but just the old-fashioned marking stitch. The squares were worked in green, the stars in yellow, and in each point of the stars were little stars, worked in different colors; and so the whole carpet was made by hand. It was real handsome when it was done. Folks came from all around to see it."

"How I wish I could have seen it, grandma! Think of working a whole carpet by hand! I have been nearly all winter doing a table-spread. But how did they get the furniture for the rooms?"

"Father started for Portland on horse-back—that was the nearest place where furniture could be bought."

"How far was it, grandma?"

"A hundred miles, and most of the way through the woods. But there was a good road, and teams always going and coming.

Father told mother to send Job along with the ox-team, after he had been gone two days. Father got home several days before Job, but at last he came with a big load of things.

There were two high-posted bed-steads, looking-glasses, tables and chairs, but what I thought was nicest of all, were two great bell-metal basins."

"What were they for?"

"They were to fill the place of the earthern wash-bowls we have nowadays. None were to be had then. Bell-metal and pewter basins were used instead.

Well, the rooms looked very nice when they were done. Mother put up some green and white checked bed-curtains, home-made, out of flax and wool, and trimmed with yellow fringe.

When court set, in November, the judges came to our house, and always after for every term of court for many years.

Now, all you have to do when you want a carpet, is to go to the store and select it; but I am sure you can never have one you can feel half so proud of as mother did of hers."

" Come, Annie," said Mrs. Belmont, entering the room, with her bonnet on, " I am ready to go now."

" Thank you, grandma, for your story. I am afraid I have lost some of my interest in buying the new carpets. I wish we could make some, as my great-grandma did."

THE DRIVE OVER PAGE HILL.

The drive over Page Hill to the Northumberland road, returning by the Beattie pine woods, a distance of seven miles, is probably less frequented than any in this vicinity. One reason is no doubt owing to the road, which is in some places rather

rough, but chiefly because the scenery in that locality is not supposed to be very attractive, at least that
is what we thought until recently, when on one
pleasant afternoon, when the sunshine was tempered
by a gentle west wind, and a shower had laid the
dust and made grass and foliage wear a fresher green,
we took this drive over Page Hill.

We leave the village by North street, and, after
crossing the railroad track, take the road leading to
the right. A few rods brings us to the house of
Mr. John W. Stevens, just at the foot of the hill.
Page Hill derives its name from Mr. David Page,
one of the first settlers of the town, and who was
the first owner of this land. This hill is not very
steep, and we soon reach the top. Looking back
toward the west, we get a lovely view of the Connecticut, winding its devious way through the green
meadows. As we go on, we pass on the right, the
farm of Mr. George H. Stalbird. A field of ripen-
ing oats, golden in the afternoon sunshine, make a
pleasant contrast with the brighter green of the sur-
rounding fields. On the left, beyond the cultivated
fields, pastures and wood-lots, are the green hills of
Vermont. Now we come to the Moore place, and
pass on the right, an orchard, the trees loaded with
apples. Just here we notice a road on the left,

which leads to the " Goodale farm." After passing the homes of Messrs. Willard and John Moore, the road is not very good, as it is but little used beyond this point. Another mile brings us to the old Daniel Spaulding place. Mr. Spaulding, the original owner of this farm, was the son of Mrs. Phebe Spaulding, a woman renowned for her courage and determination. The old house is only a ruin, and the land is owned by Mr. Horace Holton and others. Of the once large orchard, only a few trees remain, and there is but little to indicate that this was once a thrifty farm. Just beyond the old house is a great flat rock, extending nearly across the road; just here we will leave the carriage, and fasten our horse to the fence, beneath the shade of an old apple tree; then passing through some bars on the right, we walk about thirty rods through the field to a slight elevation. Ah! does not this grand view repay us? In the foreground, we look down upon thousands of acres of primeval forest, beyond that we see the Gore, Lost Nation, New France, or Parks' Mills, and rising above all, like a grand frame for this beautiful picture, is the Pilot range, flecked with shadows from the soft white clouds floating above it. The cleared land and fields of yellow grain, extending in some places half way up the mountain sides, the farm houses and mills, all contrast pleasantly with the unbroken forest. Twenty-five years ago, where we now look down upon thirty farms, there had not a clearing been made, and the only inhabitants were wolves and bears. Turning to the right, we see Mts. Prospect and Pleasant, Stebbins Hill, Hodgdon Hill, and get a glimpse of the houses of the village in the valley below. To the left, seemingly almost within our reach, are the Percy Peaks and Mt. Lyon. From this point the land in thirteen towns can be seen. Reluctantly we turn away from this charming prospect, and are soon driving on. Grass is growing in the road, indicating that it is not much traveled, and blackberry bushes, loaded with luscious fruit, bend temptingly near us. Arching boughs of golden rod, and bunches of purple asters, and elder bloom, light up the way side, and glow in patches in the fields. The land on either side of the road is rugged and rocky, but occasionally we pass a field of oats or corn, charming in contrast with the rugged scenery by its side. Over hill and down dale we go, through a wonderful web of light and shade, with a glimpse now and again of far off mountain peaks, or undulating ranges of hills, until driving down a hill rather steeper than any previous, we come out on to the

Northumberland road, just above the railroad crossing. We turn to the left, and find ourselves on a smooth, level road, and get a glimpse of the silvery gleaming of the Connecticut through the trees on the right. Very soon we enter the pine woods and inhale the delightful piney odor from the trees. Soon we pass on the left the cozy home of Captain Beattie, and a little farther on at the right, is the " Bellows Place," now owned by Captain Beattie. The old house, that has been the scene of many happy gatherings and merry makings, was fast falling into a dilapidated condition, but has been thoroughly repaired by the present owner.

We recall the delightful views afforded by this drive, we regret that the road is not in a more favorable condition, if it was, we are sure this would become one of the favorite drives in this vicinity. The remark made by a Scotchman in regard to his own mountainous country, applies to Coos County admirably: " It's a grand country. If it's nae great comfort to the purse, it's aye a pleasure to the e'e."

THE OLD CEMETERY.

To many of the residents of Lancaster, the old grave-yard is a sacred spot. There are none of the older people who have not followed the remains of dear ones through the gate and up the hill to their last resting place.

Recently in strolling through this spot where

" Each in his narrow cell forever laid,
The rude forefathers of the hamlet sleep,"

we stopped to read some of the inscriptions, that in some cases furnish facts for biography and history, which the cemeteries of our day will afford scant material, as the monuments of a recent date, do not, in some cases, impart the age of the dead and only the initials of the name are used.

In publishing some of the inscriptions, which we copied with much difficulty from the moss covered stones, that time's busy fingers will soon have entirely effaced, we do so with reverence, thinking the quaint and interesting inscriptions should not be entirely lost.

Within a small enclosure, lying flat on the ground, is a large stone bearing the two following inscriptions:

EMMONS STOCKWELL,

DIED NOV. 8, 1819, IN THE 78 YEAR OF

HIS LIFE.

One of the first settlers of this town, his descendants more than 120. Honesty and industry attended him through life.

Mark the perfect man and behold the upright, for the end of that man is peace.

RUTH,

WIFE OF EMMONS STOCKWELL.

DIED MARCH 21, 1828.

On other stones in various parts of the ground were found the following:

MRS. RACHEL,

WIFE OF CAPT. DAVID PAGE,

DIED APRIL 28, 1817.

MRS. ELIZABETH HUNNEX,

WIFE OF SAMUEL HUNNEX,

DIED 1822, AGED 63.

The last enemy that shall be destroyed is death.

IN MEMORY OF

MRS. MARY BRACKETT,

RELICT OF MR. JOSEPH BRACKETT,

DIED JULY 15, 1814. AGED 70.

In active usefulness, christian meakness and patience she was rarely surpassed.

REV. JOSEPH WILLARD,

DIED JULY 22, 1827, AGED 66 YEARS.

For 28 years pastor of the Congregational Church of this town.

JONAS BAKER,

DIED FEB. 14, 1828.

" An honest man is the noblest work of God."

ERECTED TO THE MEMORY OF

MRS. BETSY BAKER,

CONSORT OF JONAS BAKER AND ELDEST
DAUGHTER OF JONAS WILDER,
DIED IN 1801.

STEPHEN ROSEBROOK,

SON OF JAMES AND PHEBE ROSEBROOK,
DIED FEB 17, 1815, AGED 11 YEARS.

Death is a debt to nature due,
Which I have paid and so must you,
Depart my friends, dry up your tears,
Here I must lie till Christ appears.

SACRED TO THE MEMORY OF

MARY,

CONSORT OF STEPHEN WILSON,
WHO DIED FEB. 28, 1813, AGED 45.

Let sorrow change to sacred mirth,
Know God in love hath given,
The pure in heart who mourn on earth,
Perpetual smile in Heaven.

CHARLES STUART,
COUNSELLOR AT LAW,
DIED MAY 17, 1837, AGED 46.

JOHN B. ASPINWALL,
DIED MAY 25, 1833, AGED 26.

He's gone and left this world of pain,
This dark and dismal shore,
We only part to meet again,
And meet to part no more.

IN MEMORY OF
MR. NICHOLAS WHITE,
WHO DIED MAY 28, 1813, AGED 54.

Stop, traveler, as you pass by,
As you are now, so once was I,
As I am now so you must be,
Prepare for death and follow me.

ANDREW ADAMS,
DIED APRIL 14, 1833, AGED 97.

The graves of all the Saints He blessed,
And softened every bed,
Where should the dying member rest,
But with the dying Head.

This monument is erected by North Star Lodge as a tribute of affectionate respect to the memory of their deceased and worthy brother

ARA W. BURNAP,
WHO DIED UNIVERSALLY ESTEEMED AND RESPECTED,
MARCH 21, 1813. AGED 45.

www.ingramcontent.com/pod-product-compliance
Lightning Source LLC
Chambersburg PA
CBHW030539270326
41927CB00008B/1447